"What the ..."

A Conversation About Living

Darryl Bailey

NSP
united kingdom

Layout and cover design: Julian Noyce
Front cover photo: Young Darryl Bailey

ISBN: 978-1-9993535-4-4

This one conversation is composed from portions
of many conversations with my close friend,
Sally Shea Murphy.

She urged me to share them with others.
—Darryl Bailey 2019

*Questioner: I'm curious as to why you agreed to this
conversation. For some time, you've been turning down
requests to speak about your perspective on life and you
haven't written anything new for an even longer period.*

*When you stopped giving general talks, you said you had
nothing more to offer, that everything was in the books
you'd already written, and on your website.*

Darryl Bailey: Yes, but for many years, I've had people
asking me to talk about my own life journey. I've resisted
that, because each of us is unique, and the details of my
life aren't really important to anyone else's situation.
Instead, I wrote about aspects of life that are common to
all of us.

However, some people have difficulty relating to the essential points that I wrote about, feeling that they're somewhat cold and not easy to relate to in their own life situation.

Recently, a close friend has been urging me to say more about my own process, because she feels it adds something valuable to my other works, and it helped her get a fuller sense of what I'm saying.

Q: Is it something new?

DB: It's new, in that it's the details of how things occurred in my own life. It adds some practical context to my other works.

I've also been noticing how difficult it is for people to see some of the points that I've been making. Specifically, points about the limitations and contradictions of our thinking process.

Most of us are not very clear about our actual experience of life. Generally, what we think about life doesn't match our actual experience, and that confusion contains a great deal of mental, and emotional, conflict and misery.

The removal of that confusion, and misery, can come about with a very direct examination of our actual experience. There are some simple questions we can ask, to help us in that examination, and I'd like to consider some of those questions in a detailed way.

Q: *Where would you like to begin?*

DB: Well, let's start with my own particular process of exploring life, and some of the surprises that came up in the journey.

I don't want to put my life forward as a model for anyone else, because each of us is unique. I can't say exactly how life will unfold for anyone else, but I can talk about some of the things that commonly come up for anyone who is exploring life deeply; and I can say some things about my own particular journey.

Q: *That would be great.*

DB: First of all, you should know that this was a long process. The sense of existence that I have, in this moment, arose over a period of fifty-four years, with time spent in four countries, exploring various spiritual and philosophical teachings.

It started in my teen years, around the age of fourteen. It was 1965 and I was living in the center of Canada.

That period of my life was very confusing, with many conflicted thoughts and emotions, but there were moments when all of those thoughts and emotions would disappear. The thoughts and feelings would literally fall away, and the happening of the moment simply felt like one big, vibrant occurrence.

I had been experiencing those moments from the age of seven, but, by fourteen, they took on a new quality. There was a tremendous feeling of freedom, and peacefulness, in those moments, that was shockingly different from my usual feelings of confusion and conflict. It felt as though life was perfectly fine as it was, and I became fascinated with those experiences.

They seemed to promise some kind of happiness, and sense of ease, that was very different from my usual teenage angst, so I wanted to learn more about that feeling of freedom and peacefulness. I wanted to examine my shifting mind states more closely.

I was reading books by a philosopher named Jiddu Krishnamurti, and he recommended learning about life through direct observation. That made a lot of sense to me; it seemed very scientific and objective.

Back then, I believed that 'I' was separate from the rest of existence and could observe it, in order to get more understanding, so that 'I' could direct my life more skilfully.

I was fascinated by the fact that, if I sat down, or lay

down, and simply paid attention to what was happening, the happening of the moment could be explored, and that included my own physical and mental functioning.

One of the first things that really stood out was that everything was changing. Thoughts, moods, body sensations, perceptions, and so on were all dancing around. The more I simply observed and let the moment reveal itself, the more that became very obvious.

Change was also evident in the world around me. It was easy to see that everything around me was moving and shifting in some way, even though much of it was changing very slowly.

I could see change in everything that I experienced. Some things changed slowly, and some changed quickly, but everything was changing.

In some of the slower stuff, I could see that movement in time-lapse videos, of things like plant growth or the changing of seasons.

All of this felt like my own little science project, but I also heard major scientists declaring the same thing, in their observations.

In quantum physics, they declared there weren't actually any objects, there was only process, or flow. And astronomers were saying that the entire universe was a moving, evolving, event.

So, this fact of change became obvious and compelling.

Direct observing became my main method for learning about life. I became interested in meditation, exploring many different techniques that were often focusing on concentration and relaxation, but it was always to support my ongoing observation of life.

I also discovered that I could become very concentrated and sometimes experienced life with extreme intensity. I experienced bizarre states of mind that would sometimes come in those very intense moments.

Q: Bizarre? What was bizarre about them?

DB: In some of those moments, it was difficult to know if I was in the world or the world was in me.

There were moments in which I seemed to have premonitions about things in the near future. But they were sporadic, unpredictable intuitions that I couldn't really define or depend on.

There were energy releases in my body, strong currents of energy running from my feet up to my head and back down again.

My mind states would sometimes move from experiencing the body to experiencing a feeling of space and then on to a feeling of nothingness.

Those experiences matched some of the things I was reading about in meditation texts, things like Kundalini energy releases and *jhana* states. *Jhana* is the Pali word for concentration.

It was confusing, and sometimes frightening, because those experiences were so unusual, compared to my normal states of mind.

At one point, just before I left Canada to study with Ruth Denison, the concentration exercises that I was doing were extreme. I was also fasting and doing yogic breathing exercises. I was living in Vancouver at the time and, one night, I wandered away from my home, barefoot, in a trance state, with my thoughts interpreting the things around me as elements in my own mind.

I came out of that trance eight hours later, with my feet cut and bleeding, from walking over glass and stones in the street.

I was worried that I had pushed things too far, maybe doing some real damage to my brain, and I needed help. So, I went to the local hospital and had myself sedated.

The doctors were reluctant to sedate me at first, thinking it wasn't necessary, since I appeared to be fairly normal, but once they heard what I was experiencing, they did medicate me, and kept me in for observation.

I was convinced that I was losing my mind and wouldn't be coming back to sanity. That was a very frightening and lonely time.

They diagnosed me as manic-depressive, what is now known as bipolar disorder. They said I had a chemical imbalance in my blood, and suggested that I go on lifelong medication to regulate the imbalance.

In talking with three different psychiatrists, I explained that, for two weeks, I had been doing extreme concentration practices for twelve hours a day, along with fasting and yogic breathing exercises.

I asked if that could produce the confusion that I was experiencing. All of them said no.

I didn't really know what the facts were, but when they said my practices had no relationship to what I was experiencing, I wasn't sure that they really knew what this was. So, I declined their recommendations.

I did appreciate the short-term drugs that they gave me, because they helped to settle my mind. So, after a couple of weeks in an outpatient unit, sitting in a corner, almost comatose, with drool sliding out of my mouth and onto my hospital gown, things calmed down.

My mother flew to Vancouver to take me back to Manitoba. I stayed with my family for two months, until I felt well enough to leave. I've been fortunate to have a family that has always been supportive. My poor mom had to suffer through a lot of this with me.

Over the next two years, I experienced those mind states a few times, but the moment they appeared, in even the slightest way, I would stop my concentration practices and they would leave. After that, I never experienced them again.

There was a lot that I learned, in all areas of my life, but I never questioned my basic story of being someone separate from life, someone watching and learning, someone who was gaining more understanding. And I never questioned the assumption that I was directing my life.

I experienced a wide variety of situations, different schools, jobs, relationships, and that went on for about seventeen years.

Q: What kind of schools and jobs?

DB: I started working summer jobs at sixteen. My brother and I were lifeguards at a swimming pool. We would also help my father in his job; he managed a construction firm at the time. We had started out on a farm. My dad farmed in the summer and was a bush pilot in the winter, before we moved to a small city when I was about seven.

Q: *Bush pilot?*

DB: Yes. He flew in the far north of Canada; flying supplies and medical help into remote northern areas. After we moved to the city, he managed a construction firm, until he went into business with some friends. They built a hotel and a shopping mall. I would occasionally work for them, in construction.

Q: *What other things did you do?*

DB: Ahhh, let's see. I graduated high school and worked to get money for traveling. It was 1969 and teenagers were commonly backpacking though Europe. I did the same for about six months.

Over the years, I worked as a carpenter, an ice fisherman, a suit salesman, and a buyer for a fashion firm. There were social work jobs, bookstore jobs, bus driving jobs, and so on. I was paying my way through university and exploring different segments of society.

I explored different faculties at university. I did a year of general arts, then opted into social work, before landing in architecture and design, eventually getting a design degree. Design is basically problem solving, and that applies to everything. All of that schooling was in Winnipeg.

I was also moving back and forth between Winnipeg and Vancouver, investigating possible careers. I thought my investigations would last only a few years, before I would settle down, get married, and have a family.

I had heard a quote from Socrates, stating, "An unexamined life isn't worth living", and that appealed to me.

I took it to mean that, if we're going to live life, we should explore it, learn about it, so we can live it well, and I wanted to explore it thoroughly.

But it stretched on for seventeen years. I never did find any particular career and never met anyone that I wanted to marry.

Q: So, it was around that time you went to study with Ruth Denison?

DB: Yes. The process of learning about life, through direct observation, had become more fascinating, and I wondered if that was my real calling.

It seemed like I was learning a very profound psychology. By that point, I had read every book on meditation that I could find, and had found descriptions of the many states of mind that I was experiencing in romantic poetry, religious writings, and various philosophies.

I still didn't understand those moments when all of my thoughts would fall away and life felt like one moving event. I was experiencing them more often, but they never stayed, and I wasn't quite sure what that was all about.

From the age of fourteen, that falling away of thoughts seemed to be something strange about perception itself, something that I wasn't seeing clearly.

Around age thirty-one, I wanted to find someone who could help me with it, someone who knew more about it, and I was considering moving to other parts of the world to pursue it.

But that was worrisome, because it definitely wasn't following a career path and it didn't promise any pension plan. But it was my strongest interest, and everything else was unappealing.

I have to say, by that point, I was feeling really lost. I hadn't been able to find any place in society where I seemed to fit. I went through a very difficult winter, even considering suicide, before I felt compelled to follow my interest in meditation.

All of my hopes, of what my future could be, had fallen apart. I was emotionally exhausted. My time in the hospital had been incredibly confusing and depleting.

I wasn't so sure that I was actually going to survive some of it. It sometimes felt like I was barely able to crawl to the next thing that made any sense.

Q: What got you through those times?

DB: I'm not really sure. I come from a family of seasoned midwestern farmers; they had all been through very tough times. Their attitude was that, when life brings you to your knees, you then start crawling as wisely as you can.

Some of my closest friends had also gone through very difficult times. So, extreme hardship just seemed be part of life. But I was pretty fragile, both physically and mentally, for a long time.

By that point, I had become interested in the primary Buddhist meditation, called mindfulness, because it stressed a very objective observation of whatever was happening.

So, after seventeen years of exploring on my own, I went to California to study with mindfulness teacher Ruth Denison.

Ruth had a very playful approach to observing life, but a very powerful one. She wasn't stuck on any formal posture or technique; it was always the simple acknowledgment of anything that was happening in the moment, no matter what the situation.

She had very creative ways of attracting my attention to the different situations, sensations and moods of the moment. Instead of a forceful observing, she emphasized a playful curiosity.

Many people thought she was a bit kooky, but I knew that some very respected meditation masters in southeast Asia had great respect for her approach.

Renowned teachers, like Sayagi U Bah Khin, and Mahasi Sayadaw, felt that she was offering the essence of Buddhist meditation in a very powerful, natural way.

So, with her, I learned a more relaxed and fun quality to this ongoing observation of life. She taught me to be gentle with myself.

I also became less attached to my world of thought, because I realised, at one point, that ideas were an endless stream, always moving and shifting, never coming to any conclusion.

The belief that I was something separate from life also began to fade.

I had always generally thought that I was an awareness, being aware of objects that were separate from me, but I realized that awareness and the objects of awareness were basically the same thing.

For example, there's this experience that we call seeing. If we look at one of the chairs in this room, we can realize that chair is just a small part of the larger happening that we call seeing. It's the same happening, being given two different names. It seems like they're two different things, but they're not.

The observing and the thing being observed are the same essential happening. That's also true of hearing, touching, tasting, smelling, and thinking.

That was also something that Jiddu Krishnamurti was saying. In those days, I had the opportunity to hear him speak, in San Francisco and Ojai, and he would often say, "The observer is the observed."

I had never understood it when he said it, but in my meditation experience, it was becoming evident. It wasn't totally clear, but it became obvious that thought was creating a strange interpretation of life's happening, making it more complex than it actually was.

At one point, Ruth took me to see a man named Robert Adams, who was a friend of hers. He was considered by many to be an "enlightened" being.

I had read about enlightenment but didn't know what it was and really didn't have much interest in it. I was curious about it, but I was more interested in my ongoing observations of life.

I put off meeting Robert for a long time, but Ruth eventually forced me to meet him. Which was pleasant. He was an unassuming, good-natured person who had an interesting view of existence.

He would say things that were confusing, at first. Things like, "You are not the body, you are not the mind." However, in my conversations with him, he explained that he was saying something very simple.

The statements that we are not the body or mind were simply pointing out that those descriptions of life are not true.

He was emphasizing that the happening of this moment can't be defined, in any true way. It's a simple fact that we're not a body or a mind, because those are false interpretations of the unexplainable happening that we really are.

All of that made sense to me, from my own experience. I knew that, as babies, we don't understand anything and the words we have as adults are only sounds that we've been taught to bark. They don't really explain what anything actually is.

It's also the case that we use words to point to certain forms in life, like cars and houses, but those forms are always changing. Everything in existence is changing; it doesn't have any actual form that we could possibly describe.

So, I was able to relate to Robert's observations from my own experience.

I studied with Ruth for nine years. For six of those years, I was living in Oakland, California, or Berkeley, working at various jobs but, for three years, I lived at her center in the Mojave Desert, and she asked me to start teaching.

During my time in California, I was making a living any way I could. I took whatever work was available. I worked as a gardener, janitor, and woodworker, as well as a salesman in a woodworking store. For a while I took care of sexually abused children in group homes.

17

I was worried about working illegally, so my girlfriend agreed to marry me. We were together for many years. We had gotten married to make me legal, and eventually divorced, but we're still friends, even now. We helped each other through some very tough times.

When I moved to Ruth's center, I worked as her maintenance man, for room and board. I knew a little bit about a lot of things, carpentry, plumbing, wiring, and so on.

I liked the desert. I lived for a while in an abandoned trailer, and later in a small cabin on the edge of Twenty-nine Palms military base, a large area where they train American marines for desert warfare.

At night, I could watch helicopters and tracer bullets lighting up the sky above the distant mountains.

And in the mornings, I would watch coyotes and jack rabbits lope by. I loved those rabbits, with the early morning sun behind them, causing the blood in their ears to glow like lanterns.

I learned to watch for black widow spiders, whenever I went to the outhouse toilet. There was one time, though, when I sat down and heard a rattlesnake rattle. I couldn't figure out where it was, until I realised it was under the toilet seat that I was sitting on.

I basically maintained the buildings at Ruth's center. Occasionally, she gave me other jobs.

She and her husband Henry were separated, and he lived at their house in West Hollywood. They were going on holiday at one point, and she asked if I would paint the house while they were away.

She bought some remaindered cans of paint that were different colours, and told me to mix them together. She believed they would make a dark brown colour, but she never told me that.

They went on holiday and I lived at their house for three weeks, painting a large portion of it. The mixed paint colours actually made purple, not brown, so things got a bit tense when they returned.

I loved Ruth's creative approach to exploring life, but I became curious about the traditional, orthodox approach to meditation.

Nine years after I met her, she said that she had taught me everything she knew and she felt I might be suited to life in a monastery.

I had been reading the teachings of a Buddhist meditation monk named Sumedho, and flew to England to visit his community. I stayed there for six years as an ordained monk, under his guidance.

Again, there was lots to learn. That was my first experience of a big religious organization. There were the various jobs and duties that were involved in maintaining the different monasteries, in England, Switzerland, and Italy. Over the years, I worked at a number of different jobs in different monasteries.

I was Sumedho's secretary, in England, for two years. At other times, I was the guest monk, taking care of guests, or the work monk, assigning jobs.

My experience with altered states of mind was useful on long retreats, when others would start exhibiting strange behaviour. I was asked to care for them and established a connection with the local psychiatric unit.

In Switzerland, I insulated one end of the monastery. It was an old Swiss hotel that had been damaged in an avalanche, years earlier. They had capped the damaged end, but no one had insulated it. It was high up in the Swiss Alps and it got cold in the winter.

The abbot of the Swiss monastery didn't want to teach meditation, so when I arrived, he asked me to do the teaching.

I loved Switzerland. The monastery was on a lush, green alpine meadow, and the bare rock faces went straight up from there. We were five minutes walk from a hundred-foot waterfall and, at certain places, behind the monastery, we had a view of the entire valley. It was breathtaking.

It was an orthodox meditation tradition that I was in, so there was always a focus on observing whatever was happening in the moment. There was also formal sitting meditation at five in the morning, before the workday began, and, again, at seven in the evening, to end the day.

Every two weeks, we would sit in meditation through the entire night. That was the night when we recited the monastic rules.

For two months out of each year, we had a longer period of meditation and silence. The work was kept to a minimum and we would speak only when necessary.

I learned about the Buddhist rebirth teaching. I had heard of it, years earlier, but it had been explained as a reincarnation teaching. Once I got to the monastery and read the original version, it became obvious that it wasn't about reincarnation; it was a psychological teaching.

It was pointing to the false explanations that we have for

existence, the false beliefs, and the frustrations and fears that those false beliefs contain.

It was also saying that, to get free of those false ideas and beliefs, we had to pay attention to our actual experience of life.

There were many different things that I experienced in the various monasteries over the six years, but there was a growing frustration with the process of observing. It felt like I was always learning useful things, but I also felt that there were some essential things I wasn't seeing clearly.

I was still confused about those moments when thoughts would fall away and life felt incredibly whole and free from conflict.

It also became obvious that I wasn't really suited to life as a monk. There was much about the Buddhist teaching that I didn't relate to. And the political infighting that any big organisation has was difficult.

My physical health suffered. Eating only one meal a day was challenging. I normally weigh a hundred and eighty pounds and my weight had fallen to a hundred and twenty-seven.

I had also crushed the last disc in my back in a work accident, and spent a year in bed before it was surgically repaired. Everything, combined, brought my monastic life to an end.

I returned to lay life. And, after sixteen years of living in other countries, I returned to Canada. My parents were getting older and I wanted to be near them, to help, if they ever needed it.

I had been teaching meditation and, when I returned to Canada, people wanted me to continue teaching. They told me I could make a career out of being a meditation teacher, but I wasn't drawn to that.

I had been travelling around for thirty years, exploring different living situations, and I wanted to settle somewhere. I had no more urge to travel and felt I had examined enough of life.

I came back to this area of Canada where I had grown up. I found work and settled in.

Over the next year and a half, I did teach a few meditation retreats for people in this area, and a couple of retreats in other parts of North America, but eventually, I drifted away from Buddhism and meditation.

Q: How were you feeling, after leaving the monastery?

DB: I was tired. I felt worn out. I also felt like a failure. I had drifted around for so many years and there I was, at age forty-seven, starting over again, with nothing. That was in 1998.

I hadn't found any career that appealed to me more than any other, and I hadn't been able to solve the puzzle of my strange shifts in perception.

When I first started exploring, thirty-three years earlier, there weren't many books on the subject of meditation, but by the time I left the monastery, the bookstores were flooded with every spiritual teaching you could imagine, and they all had different messages.

Spirituality had become a major commercial enterprise and, by that point, I wanted to stay away from it all.

But my basic curiosity in life remained and, after a year, I began reading a variety of things, books on art, politics, economics, and so on.

My girlfriend at the time had a library of spiritual books that I wasn't really familiar with and, one day, when I was looking for something to read, I picked up one of those books.

It was written by a man named Ramesh Balsekar, student of Nisargadatta Maharaj. If I remember correctly, it was titled *Explorations Into the Eternal* and focused on the teachings of his teacher.

I read it and felt there was something significant in it, but also felt I wasn't understanding all that it was saying. It seemed complicated. I read it a couple of times.

Then, early one Sunday morning, I picked it up again. This time I read a few lines that basically said, if you consider your actual experience of life, you won't find anything to indicate that you are directing the movement of your life.

In that moment, a number of things happened. My eyes left the page, memories of my life flashed by, and my thoughts said, "You haven't done anything, ever."

It became obvious that there wasn't any actual experience of me making anything happen. There was no experience of me causing anything to happen.

Whatever I had done had been driven by urges that I hadn't created. In fact, in that moment, it became clear that I wasn't creating myself in any way at all.

I was an expression of nature, like the birds and the trees. Even my thoughts weren't my creation. Nothing, in any moment, was my creation; it wasn't my "doing".

Q: *What did that feel like?*

DB: For a second, it was exciting, then it became extremely unnerving. It was very disorienting. I kept thinking, "This can't be true."

However, it became obvious that I wasn't in any bizarre state of mind. I felt very relaxed and clear, and what I was seeing was something that was very simple to see.

As I lay there, it was obvious that I wasn't making myself happen. I could feel it.

I was happening the way that trees grow and weather changes. It just happens. And it was very easy to see and feel.

However, I didn't really trust it.

So, I lay there trying to find a mistake in what I was experiencing. But I couldn't find a mistake. It was very simple, and very obvious; I wasn't creating myself.

I was simply happening. Breath coming and going. Thoughts coming and going. Pulsations, vibrations, waves of energy. Clarity. Confusion. It was all simply happening on its own. Even that realization was happening on its own.

I realized that I didn't have to worry about anything. All of it was the movement of the universe and it was going to happen the only way it could happen.

Everything was the natural and perfect expression of existence. I wasn't anything separate from the movement of existence itself.

Existence has its own formative urge; its own way of expressing everything. If I had an urge to do something, that urge wasn't my personal creation. Nothing was my creation.

I wasn't influencing anything. It was all simply happening on its own, and that included everything that I seemed to be and do.

I realised that this was what I had been trying to get clear about, for my entire life.

This was what had always felt so strange about perception. This was the thing that had been so confusing and, in that moment, it was incredibly clear.

Those periods when all the thoughts had fallen away, and life seemed to be one big movement, were simply an experience of what was actually happening.

Those moments when it felt that there was total

freedom, were moments when the complicated stories had fallen away and the simple, automatic happening of existence made itself obvious.

But, in that particular moment, the freedom was revealing itself when the stories were present. It became clear that the stories, the thoughts themselves, were simply happening on their own.

And this experience wasn't leaving; it was staying.

As the days went by, it became even more obvious. I was amazed at how obvious it was. Why hadn't I realised this before?

I began remembering various teachings that had pointed to this, but they were always mixed with other teachings that were saying something very different.

I could remember pieces, in all the traditions and philosophies, that were saying there is only the movement of something that can't be understood.

There were specific quotes that were coming up ... "everything is Spirit" ... "the flowing of the Tao" ... "the unformed ocean of existence" ... "sitting quietly, doing nothing, spring comes, grass grows by itself".

They had all pointed to it quite clearly, but no one had really emphasized it. Instead, the focus had been on other, contradictory, teachings.

All the teachings had expressed this, in some way, but it was hidden within a larger group of teachings, focusing on the idea that we're directing ourselves through life and we always have to correct ourselves in some way.

All the teachings, that I had explored, said contradictory things. And all the years of trying to understand those contradictory statements hadn't made them less confusing.

But my actual experience of life was very simple. There was no experience of me making myself happen. There was no experience of me making anything happen.

No one had ever pointed to that as directly as Balsekar. I began looking for other individuals who were expressing the same thing, and I came across the teachings of U.G. Krishnamurti.

In particular, I ran across the transcript of a dialogue that he'd had with another person. At one point, the person he was talking to said something like, "Our thoughts direct our life", and U.G. responded by saying, "There are no thoughts".

He went on to say that we'd been taught to call them thoughts, but there's no way of saying what they really are.

As I read that, it pointed to my own sense of life being an unexplainable happening, the same thing that I had discussed with Robert Adams many years earlier. But it took on new impact.

Not only was there no thinking, there was also no seeing, no hearing, no touching, no tasting, and no smelling. Those interpretations of life are not true. There is literally no way of saying what anything actually is.

Even though I had considered that, years earlier, there had still been the feeling that I was perhaps a consciousness separate from thought, a kind of pure awareness that could exist without thought.

But, in that moment, it became obvious there could never be an awareness without thought, because the thought of "awareness" is only a thought, a false label. What "is" can never really be named or explained.

After reading those bits from Balsekar and U.G., everything I had ever experienced came down to two essential facts: there isn't any way of saying what anything actually is and I'm not making anything happen. No one is.

Everything is merely an unexplainable, unformed occurrence, moving in accordance with its unexplainable urges, and we don't exist as anything other than that.

All of my thoughts and behaviour are simply a spontaneous arising. I don't create my urge to act in any particular way. And I don't create my abilities to follow through on that urge. All of it is the happening of something that can't be explained.

At that point, some major concerns were coming up. If I didn't believe that I was responsible for my behaviour, would I start behaving in a totally irresponsible way?

If I couldn't really explain what anything actually is, would I lose the ability to communicate?

If I didn't exist as anything definable, would I lose the ability for relationship?

It all sounds ridiculous now, but this is what was coming up. The whole experience was world shattering.

Anything I had ever read made spiritual awakening sound so romantic and wonderful. It was always expressed in very romantic ways, bits of poetry and magical phrases. But all of that was ridiculous.

There is only this immediate happening that can't be explained, and it isn't being done by any so-called human being.

Then came the biggest worry. If I couldn't find a "me" making anything happen, how was anything in my life ever going to happen?

All of those worries came from my old viewpoints, the old stories, but those old stories no longer applied to my actual experience of life, so they were becoming confused.

The old viewpoint was threatened; it no longer had any evidence to support it. So, it began to fall apart. Ideas could no longer be the truth, so everything that anyone had ever said about existence was automatically being thrown out, as a truth.

It was confusing, because the so-called thoughts were still happening, but my entire process was rejecting all thought. At first, it seemed that thinking was a problem, so I didn't want to think, but thoughts were still naturally coming up.

After a while, it became clear that thinking wasn't the problem. The problem was believing the stories that thinking presented.

So, the belief that any thinking was true, ended. And the belief that the happening of life could be understood, or was being influenced, came to an end. Thinking could come and go, and it was always merely an unexplainable happening.

There was simply the feeling of everything happening in the moment, and all of it was happening automatically.

It was an unexplainable liveliness moving in accordance with its unexplainable urges. The totally free movement of something that can't be explained.

It wasn't just an idea; it was an actual feeling, the actual experience of everything happening automatically.

I remembered a poem by John Masefield, in which he had written that everything is "perpetual in perpetual change, the unknown passing through the strange".

It's difficult to say anything about it, because the descriptions are always incorrect in some way. Even what I've just been saying sounds overly romantic or poetic.

It's somehow clearer if we just ask questions. If you ask me right now what anything in this moment actually is, I would say that I don't know.

And if you ask me what's causing everything to happen the way it happens, including me, I would say I don't know: it just happens.

But that's total freedom. There's just this immediate happening, expressing itself freely, and that includes everything that I seem to be.

There's never anything to understand and never anything to really be concerned about, because it simply happens the only way it can happen. There's no option to it.

There are still the many pains and difficulties of life that arise, but there's no longer a need to understand any of it, or direct it, because there is no understanding and there never is anyone separate from it, who's directing it.

There's no feeling that any of it is incorrect; it's always the natural flow of something that can't be understood. There's no feeling of ever making a mistake in my behaviour, because I can only be what I am in any moment. I'm not creating, or influencing, any of it.

There's no feeling that anyone else is doing something wrong, because they also don't create themselves, or their behaviour.

But that doesn't mean I don't try to make life more pleasant, or that I don't try to help those in need, it's just that the urges to do those things, and the actions that come from those urges, aren't my creation. Nothing of what I am, or how I behave, is my creation.

Q: I can see that in my own life, but I'd like to make it clearer. How can I do that?

DB: I also wanted to make it clearer, but couldn't figure out how to do it.

It was as though someone had told me that there was a blue house at the end of the street, so I went down to the end of the street and, yes, it was clear, there was a blue house. There wasn't anything more to do, it was simply a fact.

Balsekar and U.G, in their writings, had told me that my experience of life was a certain way and, in looking at my actual experience, I had to agree with them; it was just as they said. It was totally clear. There wasn't anything I could do to make it clearer.

All I could do was keep checking those facts, again and again, because it just seemed too unbelievable. So I kept considering my actual experience and asking certain questions, the questions that we'll talk about at the end of this conversation.

Simply acknowledging what my experience actually was

changed everything, without really changing much of anything. All that happened was that the belief in some fantasies faded away.

But without those fantasies, life got easier. Not completely easy, but a lot easier than it had been.

Life was no longer complex and confusing; it was always simply an unexplainable happening, moving and shifting on its own.

It wasn't filled with psychological and emotional conflict. It was always simply unexplainable and happening the only way it could happen. All the beliefs that it should be happening in some other way no longer made any sense. It's just whatever it is in any moment. It can't be anything else.

The idea, that I should be something else no longer made sense. In any moment, I am what I am; nothing else is possible. I wasn't a failure any more than an ostrich was a failure or a rock.

In any moment, we are what we are, and that's always automatically moving to something else. It's the movement of something that can't be explained.

Q: So even this sense of life changes.

DB: Everything changes. This is no exception. It's gone through many shifts. For a long period, it seemed to move into deeper and deeper puzzlement.

The basic sense of everything being unexplainable, and simply happening on its own, was very clear from the start, but there were pockets of thought that still carried the old belief in understanding and doer-ship, and they would arise now and then.

But once they arose, they were seen to be false. All of the thoughts were compelled to adjust themselves to what actually is.

There was a subtle layer of doubt that lasted for a while. I even asked some of my friends to consider what I was experiencing and to tell me where I was making a mistake.

But as I was expressing the basic points to them, their own sense of life shifted.

It was obvious that the shift would occur in looking at our actual experience, but we had to look at the specific aspects that I've been mentioning.

It's possible for someone to live an entire lifetime and never look at those particular issues. In fact, most people will never look at them.

A couple of my friends were also long-time meditators, but the others weren't. None of them had ever questioned their basic story of being someone separate from life, someone who is observing and understanding life, and someone who is directing life.

With both groups, the moment that story was questioned, in a very direct way, the belief in that story could no longer exist. There was no evidence to support it.

I began rereading many of the teachings that I had explored, to see how they presented this process. They all had their own particular way of expressing it, but it was obvious they were generally saying the same thing.

Q: *What things were you reading?*

DB: It was a mix of many things. There were Zen teachings from Huang Po. Zen poetry from Ryokan. There was the Heart Sutra. I read the Bible. There was Jiddu Krishnamurti, U.G. Krishnamurti, Nisargadatta Maharaj, Alan Watts, Schopenhauer, Einstein, David Bohm, the Ashtavakra Gita, the Bhagavad Gita, Lao Tzu, and Chuang Tzu.

I read more than those, but that's all I can remember right now.

I was looking for any pieces that related to what I was experiencing, and I was able to find a few clear statements about it in almost everything I read.

Also, when I was a monk, I had written an article on the Buddha's rebirth teaching for the monastery newsletter, and it related very strongly to my new sense of existence, so I began expanding that article into a book.

That took about a year to complete and I self-published it in 2002. I called it *Buddhessence*.

My new sense of life continued to mature on its own. At one point, I became really curious as to why my attention kept coming back to thoughts as the main focus, when I knew that all of those thoughts were fantasies.

I wondered why attention wouldn't just stay with the full happening of the moment. So, in my free time, I began to notice when the focus went on thoughts and, any time that it did, I would think to myself, "false story", and also think the question, "What is there when there is no thinking?"

Every time I thought that question, what remained was the happening of the moment, without any false interpretation.

After a while, whenever the focus went on thoughts,

the question became "What actually is?" Again, when I would think that thought, all that remained was the immediate happening of the moment, without any thought trying to interpret it.

The thoughts always came back, as a natural movement of the moment, but the focus wasn't primarily on them. The focus was on the unexplainable, unformed happening that everything actually is.

One day, the attention stopped returning to thought as the main focus, and remained with the entire happening of the moment. After that, even when the focus had to go on thought, there was no urge for it to remain there when it wasn't needed.

I became less interested in thought. Whenever it was needed, I could use it, but when it wasn't needed, it just rattled around in the background and I had no interest in it. It was much more interesting to simply feel the full happening of the moment, occurring on its own.

I could even play with thought, for entertainment, but it never again presented itself as an explanation of existence. Life was always an unexplainable happening presenting itself, and the focus was primarily on that.

There were some strong emotions that shifted in surprising ways. One of them was a very deep sense of loneliness that would arise once in a while.

My life, at that time, was very full and generally pleasant, but a strong feeling of loneliness would come up every Sunday afternoon, between the hours of one o'clock and five o'clock.

It was strange, but, every Sunday afternoon, that feeling of loneliness would arise, and once it was there, it seemed like it was never going to leave. I had been experiencing it for many years.

I had always tried to understand it, because I felt that understanding it might make it go away, but it never did. With my new sense of things, I realized that there was no way to understand it.

I stopped thinking of it as loneliness. Like everything else, I really didn't know what it was, but it only ever stayed for an afternoon, so it didn't seem to be anything to worry about. I started to simply feel it, without trying to understand it, label it, or make it go away.

The moment I did that, it became difficult to feel that it was unpleasant. It was simply an intense energy. That's the way I experienced it over the next few months and, eventually, it just stopped happening.

Various frustrations with life also began to fade.

41

Existence was a movement that I wasn't influencing in any way, so it didn't make sense to fight it or get annoyed with it.

Most of my moments of frustrated anger disappeared, but it also became clear that not all of them would fade away, because some were needed for survival. An extreme irritation with certain situations is needed for moving to healthier ones.

My frustrations with other people began to fade. They weren't creating who they were, or how they were behaving, so I stopped thinking that they should be anything other than who they were.

I would often explore whether someone was open to new thoughts, or new behaviour, but, if they weren't, that wasn't because they were choosing to be stubborn.

Everyone has to think whatever they think, and behave in whatever way they behave, because that's the universe moving to its inherent nature. Asking someone to be different is like asking rain to fall up.

But that didn't mean I never got frustrated with other people. No matter how much I could see that all of us are simply the movement of the universe, some people are so different from my expression that their behaviour will always be an irritation to me.

My notions of death evaporated. In actual experience, there is only an unexplainable, vibrant occurrence, so the usual stories of birth and death stopped making any sense.

However, I still feel the pain of losing a loved one. Even the Buddha felt sorrow when he lost a friend.

Prior to this sense of things, if someone had asked me about myself, I would describe my life in the best way possible, even making it sound more special than it was. There was a sense of pride in some of the things I had accomplished.

Once it was clear that I could never truly explain existence, and wasn't causing any of it, not only did I lose my ability to define myself, in any true way, but when I was using words, I lost the ability to define myself as anything special. I'm a simple expression of nature, like everything else.

I'm doing what every expression of existence is doing, simply being the only expression I can be. Nothing more and nothing less. I'm perfectly fine as the ordinary happening that I am.

Stories of enlightenment usually carry a sense of specialness that is very misleading. None of this is about meditation and enlightenment. It's about something that can't be understood and isn't being accomplished by anyone.

Every apparent thing is compelled to be what it is. A rock is compelled to be a rock. A squirrel is compelled to be a squirrel. Any human being is compelled to be what they are in any moment. There isn't anything wrong with it.

One of the friends whom I was sharing this with is a woman named Sandra Stuart, who teaches yoga. After having her own sense of life shift, she asked if I would teach this at her yoga studio.

My initial response was to say no, because I couldn't imagine the general public wanting to listen to this kind of thing. But she convinced me to try it, just to see what would happen.

We arranged a course that would take place over seven Sunday mornings, three hours each morning. I felt it was going to be the one and only course that I would ever be presenting.

I knew that it hinged on how clearly everyone looked at their actual experience, so I focused on a very gentle but constant consideration of what our common experience actually is.

That first course had twenty-four people in it and, by the

end of the session, six of them had radical shifts in their sense of existence.

One man said he felt like he'd been infected by a happiness virus. A woman who had been dealing with the trauma of early childhood abuse reconciled with her family, after not speaking to them for fifteen years.

Anyone who experienced a major shift was confused by what was happening, because all we had done was look at our very simple experience of the moment.

The woman who had reconciled with her family told me a few weeks later that she'd been in therapy for fifteen years and nothing major had shifted, but after simply listening to what I was saying, on those Sunday mornings, all of her issues had been resolved.

I was more surprised than anyone else; it was pretty difficult to believe what was happening.

I could see that it didn't happen with everyone. Everybody could examine what I was pointing to but, for some, it was simply a curious thing, while others experienced a major shift in their entire sense of existence, and it made their lives much easier.

So the seven-week sessions continued, and, in each session, certain people's lives changed in a radical way.

The people in the gatherings began asking what they could read once the course was over, something to remind them of the major points, but I didn't know of any book that focused on the things that I was presenting. So I began writing something that would.

One of the people who had been in my first course, a man named Link Phillips, had become a friend, and was also a friend of Sandra's. I showed them what I had written. They liked it and wanted to help with it, so, with Sandra as my editor, and Link as my layout designer, we produced a book, titled *Essence*, which I again self-published. It was only for people in my sessions.

After that, everything settled into a simple routine.

My life was still presenting itself as usual, all of my needs, interests, and concerns, and all my responses to those motivating factors, were still occurring. My so-called thoughts were still arising, and they were there whenever I needed them. My sense of caring for family members and friends, and my sense of responsibility within society, was still presenting itself. But it was more obvious than ever that I wasn't creating any of it.

It felt, more and more, that life was a totally mysterious happening simply occurring on its own.

Even the process of making a decision was a process that occurred on its own; I didn't make it happen.

There were natural worries that came up in the course of any day, but I wasn't creating them. And all the appropriate responses to those worries would also come up, automatically.

I still cared about things, sometimes passionately, without really caring how any of it would ultimately play out, because none of it was my doing, not even my own behaviour.

I would always act in a way that seemed appropriate, the way that made most sense to me, but I wasn't creating my sensibilities.

There were moments when the worries and responses seemed to be confused, like a big storm. But if I just waited, they all settled down and the important aspects automatically became clear.

I continued to read various spiritual and philosophical writings that pointed to what I was experiencing but, in each book, I would find only a few clear statements about it.

My friends would sometimes laugh at me, because I would take a pen and literally scribble out everything in a two-hundred-page book, except for two lines that were clear.

Most of those books presented viewpoints that were contradictory. So, with any book, I would pick out the bits that were in agreement with my actual experience, and throw away the rest.

My favourite pieces came from Alan Watts, U.G. Krishnamurti, Albert Einstein, Jiddu Krishnamurti, and Nisargadatta Maharaj.

Most of their books had hundreds of pages describing life in a very complex way, and urging everyone to become something more than what they were. But then, in a few lines, they would also state that there was no way of saying what anything really is and that nobody is directing the course of their life.

From my actual experience, anything other than those two points seemed to be incorrect, or overly complicated, and my interest in reading anything spiritual or philosophical eventually came to a complete end.

The seven-week sessions continued, but changed to individual sessions on Sunday afternoons. Anyone who was interested could come to them and we would simply discuss our common experience of life.

I had settled into a warehouse job and my ongoing
relationships with family and friends. Life was pleasant.
I enjoyed reading about world events, art, science,
technology, and economics. I went for long walks
along the rivers that I lived close to, and got involved
with various things around town. I was free to explore
whatever interest I had.

About three years after I self-published *Essence*, I was
compelled to express my experience in a different way,
and would wake up in the middle of the night to write.
Soon, I had another book. Again, Sandra and Link
helped, and I self-published *Dismantling the Fantasy* in
2007.

My books are short, but each line, each word, is carefully
considered. It took a fair bit of time to feel out what I was
wanting to say and exactly how to say it. I was driven to
try many different approaches, before finding the one
that felt right.

Those books are stripped down to the bare essentials.
They point to everyone's most basic experience of life
and what it indicates. They're written in a language
that the average person can relate to; they don't have the
jargon that most books on this subject contain.

Almost three years after *Dismantling* came out, someone
sent my books to Joan Tollifson, who then sent them to

Julian Noyce at Non-Duality Press. And Julian asked if he could publish them.

I had written three books, but didn't offer *Buddhessence* for general publication; what I wanted to present was different than Buddhism. I also reworked *Essence*, to remove some unnecessary parts, and Sandra suggested calling the new version *Essence Revisited*.

So, *Dismantling the Fantasy* came out in 2010, and *Essence Revisited* in 2011, as publications of Non-Duality Press.

Soon after that, Marcus Fellowes contacted me. Marcus was a website designer, and had read the books. He found them helpful and, in appreciation, offered to create a website for my presentation.

Everything was going well, but I was experiencing a growing anxiety around some of it. My life in Winnipeg had been so quiet, for over ten years, and I was finally in a place where I belonged. I was afraid of losing that situation, if the books and website brought a lot of attention.

But I wanted to share my perspective, since it was helping people, so I waited to see what would happen. It did get attention but, fortunately, few people want to hear the kind of radical statements that I make.

About a year after that, Marcus wondered if I would travel to Britain to give some talks. There were people there who had an interest in what I was presenting.

By then, I had been interviewed by Urban Guru Café, a fairly popular website, and Marcus felt that I would have an audience, if I wanted to come to London.

I still didn't have any urge to travel, but was happy that what I was offering was helping people, and agreed to the trip.

Again, people experienced big changes in their lives. Many who had been on a spiritual quest for most of their lives told me later that their search came to an end, in that week of talks.

It was a powerful experience, and exhausting. I found that I wasn't prepared for the emotions of all the people who came, and spending that much time discussing very intense issues was wearing.

During that trip, I was also interviewed by ConsciousTV.

After that, I returned to Winnipeg, to let the whole experience digest, at its own pace.

Q: So you went back to your job in the warehouse?

DB: Yes, I enjoyed that work and it gave me a certain amount of freedom, for my ongoing consideration of life.

One of the big things that was occurring, after reading Balsekar and U.G., was a consideration of where real contentment could be found. Up to that point, everything that I had encountered stressed the idea that we are in charge of our lives, and we have to move ourselves to happiness and contentment, by pursuing the things that most people generally pursue.

The various philosophies and psychologies always presented an idea of what a healthy human being, or an awakened human being, is, and stated that we had to do various practices or therapies, to turn ourselves into that kind of human being. Instead of being a normal human being, there was the belief that we had to become a special human, an ideal human being.

Basically, everyone was telling everyone else what they were supposed to be.

Even the most loving spiritual teachers gave the impression that it wasn't okay for you to be what you were. They gave the impression that they had some secret knowledge of what you were supposed to be, and they would help you get to it.

From my actual experience of existence, all of those ideas

and standards became ridiculous.

Existence expresses itself in endless variety. No two snowflakes are ever identical. No two things anywhere are identical, so the idea that two people should be the same, or find contentment in the same way, or even have the same sense of existence, was absurd.

Each of us is unique. We have to be the differently unique expression that we are, and no other person knows what we're supposed to be, or what we're supposed to be doing in life. There's simply the movement of existence, expressing each apparent person in a different way.

The situation of someone telling other people what they should be, is perversely ignorant of life itself. It makes no sense. For one person to say that there's something wrong with the rest of us, is like someone stepping out under the night sky and saying that the stars aren't arranged properly. It's moronic.

People generally overlook the fact that they aren't creating their thoughts or their actions. We will think whatever thoughts nature expresses, and act in whatever way nature expresses, because we don't exist as anything other than the movement of nature.

For each apparent person to find his or her fulfilment,

they will have to feel out what is important for them, in their unique situation.

We each get our different set of needs, interests, and concerns, along with a different set of abilities and lack of abilities. There are some things that seem to be common to all of us, but even those are somewhat different for each one of us.

There is the occasional philosophy or therapy that acknowledges this wide variety in life's expression, but most are trying to force a particular standard on everyone. They want us to conform to one personality, one way of behaving, or one way of looking at life.

They have their ideas of what a perfect human being is, but that standard is impossible for everyone to meet, because we're all different.

People have their various gurus and messiahs who they feel are the model for all of humankind, the perfect person. But, as U.G. used to say, messiahs are called messiahs because they leave a big mess behind them, wherever they go.

Most therapies, that seem to help in many ways, are very judgmental. From their point of view, we are all substandard and need to be improving ourselves.

But, in any moment, we're an expression of the universe, and can't be anything more than what we are. All of it is the expression of something that can't be understood. Our contentment, therefore, lies in being whatever we are, focusing on whatever is important to us, in our unique situation, our unique expression.

However, that isn't easy to do in human society, because everyone is telling us what to be and what to do. Family, friends, the educational system, the government, spiritual leaders, therapists, and so on, are all telling everyone what to be and how to behave.

But each of us is different. Since each of us is unique, it's only in pulling away from everyone else's opinion, and feeling out our own needs, interests, and concerns, exploring the things that are meaningful to us, that we find the fullness of our own expression, and our particular wholeness.

I began being incredibly honest with myself about my own particular needs, interests, and concerns. I would acknowledge, as clearly as I could, what my feelings were in any situation. I began to notice what I could live with and what I couldn't.

It didn't matter what anyone else was doing, or what they said I should do. No matter what they said, I had my own sense of what felt healthy and what didn't.

At a certain point, I was starting to feel pressure from the people who liked my books and website. They were asking why I was still living in Winnipeg. They were saying I should be living in a big spiritual center, like California, where I could become a really well-known teacher.

They asked why I wasn't marketing myself in a bigger way; I should be asking for more money at my gatherings. I should be travelling the world, building a bigger following. I should be talking about pure awareness. I should be offering spiritual practices for people to do.

The same people who had labelled me as a nondual teacher, were now telling me that I wasn't saying the things that a nondual teacher should say.

Some of them began warning others that what I was saying was dangerous, that it was an incomplete teaching.

The really weird thing was that I had never called myself a nondual teacher. All I had ever done was point to a few facts about everyone's experience.

Within a short period of time, I realised I didn't have any urge to do what the others were pushing me to do. My own contentment didn't lie in that direction. Those things didn't have any meaning for me; they didn't make any sense.

The public has a tendency to fixate on what they consider to be acceptable, as opposed to what they think is unacceptable.

There's a great Zen story about this, in which a Zen master is dying and expressing the fact that he doesn't want to die. His students are confused, and appalled, by that, because he's a great Zen master, and they think he shouldn't be feeling the things that he's feeling. They're caught in their conflicted fantasies.

But the Zen master is free. He's free to be a natural expression of existence, the unique expression that he is. He's ultimately fine with dying, but he's also fine with not wanting to die, because both are expressions of nature; they're not his personal doing. He's content with life, as it actually is, as it actually presents itself.

People are what they are and feel what they feel. Each person is different. All of it is the movement of something that can't be explained and it simply happens the way it happens.

Over the next years, I accepted a few more invitations to be interviewed, but turned down most of them. I felt that, since I was already featured on some very respected sites, people would hear of my books and website, so no other interviews were really needed.

I had no interest in making my living out of travelling and giving talks. I received invitations to almost all the major cities in the world, and I appreciated that, but the idea of spending my life drifting around the world wasn't very appealing. And it wasn't necessary for sharing my perspective.

The website that Marcus and I had put together was getting a great response, so I focused on sharing my perspective there, where it could reach people without requiring me to travel.

I did give a series of talks throughout California at one point, and made a few more trips to the UK, before giving it up.

With the website, I was responding to people from around the world. For about five years, I was responding to questions they sent in, but the questions eventually became repetitive and I felt that, by focusing on those questions, I wasn't able to focus on other points that were important.

So I dropped the questions, and spoke about whatever I felt compelled to consider, at the end of each month.

After six and a half years, I felt I had said everything that I could say and it was all there on the website, for anyone who wanted to explore it. My books were also being sold internationally.

Both Marcus and I had other interests, taking us in different directions. So I stopped adding anything new to the site. I also stopped holding my gatherings in Winnipeg.

The things that I've been saying are not new. People have been saying similar things for the last three thousand years, according to so-called history.

Most of the great innovators that I've read about, in all areas of life, had this sense of existence, and I can find it expressed in most of the world's religions and philosophies.

It isn't necessary for me to promote this perspective in any strong way, because it has already been promoted in many different ways, some clear, some not so clear, for all of recorded history.

There are always people who seem to benefit from it and, for them, I've presented my perspective, but the vast majority of people will not be interested in it. Throughout history that's always been the fact.

It's also the case that human beings can never totally agree in their views, because each of us is different.

Even the people who say that ultimately existence is unexplainable get into arguments about it.

Just look at science and religion. One says there's a mysterious, unexplainable flowing, called energy, that is the basis of everything; and the other says there's a mysterious, unexplainable, flowing, called Spirit, that is the basis of everything. Then they argue about whose mysterious, unexplainable flowing is the right one.

By the fifth year of the website, I no longer had much interest in thought, and the act of returning to a strong focus on words was becoming more difficult.

People wanted me to continue focusing on stories about existence. Most of them wanted me to give them a formula for living life.

But from my sense of things, thought can never describe what actually is, and any time the focus goes on thought, there's less focus on what actually is.

The mysterious occurrence of this moment expresses itself a certain way, and thoughts are simply a small portion of this expression. Thought is an expression of life; it doesn't direct life.

If someone wants a formula for living, I would say do whatever you're compelled to do in any moment, because that's all anyone is doing, and that's all anyone can do. We're simply an unexplainable event moving in accordance with its unexplainable urges.

As things have moved and shifted, I've felt an ever-growing contentment in simply being whatever I am in each moment. There's no longer any standard for my behaviour, other than what I'm compelled to be and do in any moment.

That doesn't mean that I follow any whim that comes along. It's always a situation of mixed urges counterbalancing each other, until one pushes itself forward as the strongest, and that's what I'm compelled to do.

There's a piece in the Buddhist scriptures, describing some of the Buddha's enlightened followers. It says that those enlightened beings did only what they had to do. But one of the things they had to do was skip over every puddle of water that they saw.

That really confused me, when I first read it. Why would enlightened beings, who did only what they had to do, be compelled to skip over every water puddle that they saw?

It went on to explain that those enlightened beings were young children, and it immediately became obvious why they had to jump over every puddle. Because that's what nature makes children do. Jumping over puddles is great fun.

People have been telling other people how to live for thousands of years, but all anyone can ever do is follow the things that are meaningful to them, in whatever way makes sense to them. That's different for every so-called person.

I don't know what life is and I don't know why anything happens the way it does.

I do know, from direct experience, that words aren't explaining what anything actually is, and that we aren't creating anything, or influencing anything.

We're the happening of something that can't be understood. And it simply happens spontaneously.

Is it going to be pleasant all the time? No. Will it always move the way we want it to move? No. Will we always behave in some perfect way? No.

Christ was nailed to a cross. The Buddha had such extreme back pain that he often couldn't finish a teaching. Chögyam Trungpa was an alcoholic. U.G. Krishnamurti was obnoxious. Jiddu Krishnamurti was extremely argumentative. Ramana Maharshi died from a painful cancer.

All of that is the natural expression of existence. It is what it is. But it's always a mixed bag of things, and a great deal of it is incredibly wonderful, beautiful, and blissful.

This sense of life doesn't make everything constantly wonderful. It's acknowledging that life is a wide range of apparent things, and none of it is our doing.

When we believe that we're in charge, believing that we move the universe, then nothing is ever good enough. It's never what we want it to be, and we always seem to be failing to make it what it should be.

In realising that we aren't in charge, we may begin to appreciate that so much of life is wonderful, and we haven't done anything to create that. It's a gift, to be appreciated.

It's an incredible adventure, with a rich blend of experiences. One day up, another day down. Never standing still. There's no way of saying what it is.

Q: *Do you still meditate?*

DB: Meditate? I'm not sure what you're asking?

Q: Do you still sit quietly on a regular basis, to see life more clearly?

DB: No, it's not like that any more. There's no me that has to see anything more clearly. There is always only an unexplainable happening simply expressing itself in whatever way it does.

But there's often the urge to sit quietly. For me, that's something enjoyable.

Q: So where does your life stand at this moment?

DB: I'm sixty-eight years old. I'm retired from work. Over the last couple of years, I've been helping family members with health issues. At the moment, though, everything on that front is quiet.

I connect with family and friends on a regular basis. I get out for long walks by the rivers. My focus has gone on painting, for the last while. My university degree, from thirty-nine years ago, was in design, but I had a strong interest in painting and that interest has resurfaced.

My books are out in five languages, and the website is still active. People send questions, once in a while, and I respond by email. Most often, people send words of appreciation for what I've presented.

Occasionally, someone wants to skype with me. What I express in my books, and on the website, is clear, but sometimes people want to talk something over.

Q: Do you miss the kind of adventure that your life was?

In other conversations, you mentioned a gun fight that took place near your cabin in the desert, and a tornado that you were caught in. There was also a time when you were an ice fisherman, and the ice you were on had broken off and was drifting away from shore. For years you lived on the edge of oceans, or in the middle of forests and deserts, or high up in the Alps.

Your life, now, seems pretty dull, compared to that.

DB: All of that was fine when it happened, but I don't miss it.

These days, I'm living the life that is most meaningful to me, in a way that makes most sense to me. Others may look at it and think it's boring, or think I should be doing something else, but that's their way, not mine.

Q: You mentioned some questions that would be helpful in a direct exploration of life. Do you still want to talk about those?

DB: Yes, we can get into those, if you want. But I should

mention that they are a very direct examination of our experience and people may find them challenging.

Q: Okay. We are forewarned. What do you want to start with?

DB: I'd like to start with something more basic than our stories.

When people usually consider life, they start with a focus on their storylines. We have so many ideas about what life is and what it should be, as well as ideas about what we are and what we should be.

We usually focus on stories of a past and a future, thinking about past accomplishments or failures, and imagining what we want to accomplish in the future.

We have the belief that, by thinking, we understand ourselves and existence, and that, with this understanding, we're putting our life together.

We're always trying to get more understanding, by focusing on more thoughts, in order to get more control, to make life move in the direction we want it to move.

Q: Yes. I've spent most of my life doing that.

DB: That's what most of us do for most of our lives.

However, if we really want to explore life, it has to be a consideration of something more basic than thinking. The actual happening of this moment is not a thought.

This happening that we usually call seeing, hearing, touching, tasting, smelling, or thinking is not a thought. Even if we don't give it any name or description, it still makes itself obvious.

It's just this immediate feeling of being, or existing.

We normally think about this occurrence as two happenings, the outside of us and the inside of us, but it's not two things.

If we don't focus on a thought that says it's two happenings, it simply feels like one happening. The outside of me is happening at the same time as the inside of me.

If we consider what we actually experience, it's simply the feeling that something is happening right now.

So here it is, this most basic feeling of existing, and I would like to explore this with a series of simple questions. Each question is asking us to consider what our actual experience is.

I'll go through the questions quickly, but for anyone

who wants to explore this, they really need to set aside
a period where they can explore the questions at length,
and consider them thoroughly.

There may be some surprises in this exploration,
and some of it may be confusing. But it's a simple
examination of our experience and any confusion about
it won't last.

First Question

The first question I want to ask is, "What does this happening feel like? Does it feel like a past, a present, or a future?"

From your actual experience, what does this immediate feeling of existing feel like?

It's a simple question and it has a simple answer, in everyone's experience. It feels like now. It doesn't feel like a past or a future; it feels like what we call now.

We can ask this question hundreds of times, and it always feels like "now". That's our only experience. It never feels like a past or a future.

If we think about the past, that's happening now. If we think about the future, that's happening now.

There is no actual experience of a past or a future. Our only experience is the feeling of what we call now.

We don't need to meditate or do spiritual practices to realize this. We don't need to ask an expert to tell us the answer. Just ask yourself what your experience actually feels like.

If you explore this, you'll realize why both Einstein and Stephen Hawking stated that time is an illusion. It's because there's no actual experience of a past or a future; there are only ideas about them.

To believe that there's a past or a future is like believing in pink unicorns.

If I ask someone, "Do you believe that pink unicorns exist?", they would say no, because they've never experienced pink unicorns. Yet even though we've never experienced a past or a future, we generally believe that they exist.

In fact, we generally believe there's a past that is creating this present moment, even though we never experience that.

Second Question

The second question we can ask is also very simple.

"Is it possible to say what this immediate, vibrant happening actually is? Is it possible to know what any of this actually is?"

If we consider this, it's relatively easy to see that the answer is no, we can never say or know what anything actually is.

We have a bunch of words that we've been taught to bark by our parents and by society, but none of those words can really tell us what anything is.

We can point to this portion and call it a wall, or we can point to this portion and call it a neck, but those aren't a true name for anything. They're just labels that we've agreed to use for pointing to different bits of life.

In a country that speaks a language other than English, the labels are different.

If we all agreed to it, we could use letters, like x, y, and z, instead of names. So, instead of talking about bodies, consciousness, and awareness, we could talk about x, y, and z.

It's obvious that making those sounds doesn't explain what anything actually is.

We all have a story that says, when we were babies, we didn't know what anything was and our parents taught us the names for everything.

But our parents simply taught us to bark certain sounds. They taught us to bark the sounds that they were taught to bark, when they didn't know what anything was.

If I point to the wall and ask a newborn baby, "What is this?", the baby isn't going to say anything. The newborn doesn't know what anything is, in the same way that we didn't know what anything was when we were that same age.

Just because we can now point to some portion of this happening and bark a certain sound, doesn't tell us what anything really is.

We don't even know what these names and labels are.
We were taught to call them names and labels. If I
teach a seal to bark when I point to something, it isn't
explaining existence. And neither are we.

It's also the case that we focus on various patterns,
various forms, in order to explain everything.

We focus on a certain ephemeral form and call it a car.
Or a certain ephemeral form and call it an emotion.
After a while we get the impression that life is made up
of a number of different forms, or "things".

However, in our actual experience of life, we have the
impression that everything is changing. We can see that
all apparent forms move and shift and alter in some way.
All of it is movement.

It doesn't matter if we're a football player or a physicist:
one of the most common things that any human being
says about existence is that it's always changing.

So, not only do we not have a true name for anything,
but the forms we use to describe existence don't really
exist, since they're always changing.

In our actual experience, existence doesn't have any
particular form.

If we just sit here for a while, we'll notice all kinds of things that are changing. Sounds, thoughts, moods, feelings, urges, pulsations, vibrations, the shifting of the body, and so on.

Just look in the mirror and see the changes that have occurred. You used to be the size of a pea in your mother's womb. Now you're this size. And it's still shifting.

If we look at anything in existence, it's moving to another appearance.

To describe this movement as a bunch of forms is like taking a photograph of flowing smoke and saying that snapshot is an accurate picture of smoke. It's not. The photo appears to have form; the flowing smoke doesn't.

The stories that we have about existence are composed of labels that aren't any true name, placed on forms that don't actually exist, because they're always changing.

We make a lot of effort to explain existence in terms of name and form, when actually, in our experience, we don't have any true name for anything and existence has no lasting form.

These descriptions of existence are what we call understanding and knowledge, and it's a simple fact that all understanding, all knowledge, is essentially a distorted fantasy.

Those distorted fantasies can be useful in certain situations, but they are always a false impression of life.

Any time the focus goes on thinking, it's going into a fantasy.

Q: But we can't stop thinking. We need to think in order to live.

DB: I'm not saying that we should stop thinking, but it's important to see what thinking can do and what it can't do.

It can help us build a bridge, or make a meal, but it can't explain what anything really is.

Descriptions are always translating life's movement into false ideas of form, with names that aren't any true name.

This immediate feeling of liveliness, the happening of this moment, can't really be explained in terms of name and form, and we don't have any other way of saying what it is. We can't even call it "now".

The stories that we have are always some false, distorted

interpretation of what's actually happening.

These views can be helpful. We use them every day, in useful ways. We can use them as a tool, for everything from entertainment to travelling into space. But they're always, ultimately, a false description of what's happening.

Third Question

Since we're considering this, we might also ask, "What is there when there isn't any distorted interpretation?"

Since any thought is a distorted interpretation, the question can be simplified to, "What is there when there is no thinking?"

Just think that question, and see what happens. Think it a few times and, each time, simply rest at the end of the thought.

At the end of the question, there isn't any thinking. But it's not nothingness.

Notice how quickly the focus wants to come back to thinking, instead of simply resting without a story, without a fantasy.

Instead of simply resting as this immediate happening, without explanation, there's a tremendous urge to focus on thought, on fantasy.

We're not trying to get rid of thought in this consideration. It's simply that the focus is shifting away from the false stories, the false descriptions, to something more essential. It's shifting to what actually is.

Thinking is part of the happening of this moment, but only a small part. When we drop the focus on false interpretations, the full, vibrant happening makes itself obvious.

Thoughts will naturally come back as a portion of this happening. But the focus will be on the full happening and not just the thinking.

When thinking does come back, we can perhaps remember that there's no way of saying what it is. Someone told us to call it thinking, but we don't really know what it is.

What "is" is simply this immediate and unexplainable occurrence.

Fourth Question

So, again, the only actual experience we have is this feeling that something is happening now, just this immediate, unexplainable occurrence.

And the next question we can ask is, "Am I making anything happen? In this immediate happening, right now, am I making anything happen?"

It doesn't require a lot of effort to answer this.

In fact, it's just the opposite. If we sit down, or lie down, and make no effort to do anything, it becomes obvious that everything continues to happen on its own.

If you make no effort to do anything, the happening of this moment continues to happen, and that includes the happening that you are.

Q: Yes, but there are other times, when I'm very active, and it does seem like I'm making things happen.

For instance, if I want a pizza, I can initiate the actions to get that pizza.

DB: Yes, it seems like we're initiating the actions to get that pizza, but my question goes deeper, to ask if there really is an experience of us initiating that action.

In that situation with the pizza, it seems like we're initiating the process, but the question is whether we really are doing that.

If we examine that situation closely, we can see that we don't create the desire for pizza; it simply comes up, like all of our wants and needs.

Schopenhauer pointed this out in the late 1800's. He stated that we can do what we want, but we don't create our wants.

So we may want a pizza, and we may want it enough to go get a pizza, but we're not creating that want. The want is an independent, spontaneous arising. In other words, we're not deciding to go get a pizza; we're compelled to go get a pizza.

If we examine any situation where we've apparently done something, we'll discover that we were compelled to do it, either by some desire that was strong enough to push us in that direction, or by some set of circumstances that forced us in that direction.

Even if it didn't seem that we were pushed by a strong urge to do something and we simply followed an idea that popped into our head, we didn't decide what idea would pop into our head.

If I ask you to think of two animals, right now, two animals will pop up in your thoughts. But you don't decide, beforehand, which animals will pop up. That simply happens.

If I ask you to focus on only one of those animals, your focus goes to one of them, without you deciding which one.

If there is a mental debate about which one to focus on, you don't decide to have that debate.

And, out of that debate, when the focus eventually does go to one of them, it's because you simply want to focus on that particular one. But you don't create that want.

Right now, you're happening. The entire process that you are is happening. What are you doing to make yourself happen the way that you happen? The answer is very simple. Nothing.

Einstein read Schopenhauer's statement at the age of seventeen, and, in considering his own experience, realised that he was an expression of nature, like everything else.

He would eventually say that he didn't decide his existence or his behaviour, any more than a tomato plant decides its existence or its behaviour.

And that's our experience too, but few people want to admit it.

Q: *It's a scary thing to consider.*

DB: Yes, that was my feeling too, that it was frightening to consider, but as I pointed out in my own apparent journey, there are a lot of positive things that can come with this kind of exploration.

Getting back to the point, it's fairly simple to see that we don't create the urges that provoke our actions. But we also don't create the ability to act.

We don't create our body and brain, and we're not making them function the way they function. We don't create our ability to move.

Even if we have an urge to refine our abilities, like wanting to get better at playing a certain sport, we don't create that urge to get better and we don't create our ability to play better. We either have the ability to play better, or we don't.

Lots of people would like to play basketball like Michael Jordan, or play the piano like Mozart, and they work very hard at it, but very few have that ability. They don't create their interest in playing better and they don't create their potential to improve.

Q: Yes, that makes sense from my own experience.

DB: All I'm doing is pointing to our actual experience.

Q: And I agree with everything that you've pointed to. So, if we add all of it together, it's indicating that all that's ever happening is the immediate happening of the moment. There's no way of saying what it really is, and we don't exist as anything apart from it. We don't cause ourselves to happen. All of it simply happens on its own.

DB: Yes, that's it, from our actual experience. And I'd like to pick up on the last point you mentioned, to focus on one other question.

Q: Okay.

Fifth Question

DB: Since it's fairly straightforward to see that there is only this immediate happening that can't be understood, and that we aren't making anything happen, including us, we can now ask another question.

"If I'm not making any of this happen, how exactly is it happening?"

Q: It moves and shifts on its own. At least, that's what it's doing in my experience.

DB: Yes, mine too. In fact, that's what it's doing in everyone's experience.

Again, if you sit quietly, or lie down, and make no effort to do anything or think anything, it becomes obvious that everything simply happens on its own.

There are pulsations, vibrations, warmth, coolness, lightness, heaviness, twinges, body shifts, sights, sounds,

touches, tastes, smells, thoughts, moods, emotions, urges
… everything in this moment is happening on its own.

At some point, the urge to move will come up, and we
will move to some other activity. All of that simply
happens. There's no experience of a "me" making that
happen.

More than that, it's obvious that it has no particular
form. Whatever seems to be happening now is changing,
moving on to some other appearance. It's a flowing event
of some kind.

As the early Taoists pointed out, there is only this
flowing, and the way that it flows.

However, even though this flowing has no particular
form, it appears to have form. Just look around. Even
though everything is actually changing, much of it is
changing slowly, so it appears to have form.

It may also become obvious that no two forms are
identical.

Scientists will tell us that no two things are identical, but
we can generally see that in our daily lives; each thing is
basically different from every other thing.

Even in things that seem to be the same, if we examine

them very closely, we'll find differences.

No two trees, no two leaves, no two moments, no two people, and so on, are exactly the same. Some may be very similar, but they're never identical. Not even any two snowflakes are identical.

So, not only is this happening always moving and shifting, it's always expressing something different, something new.

In the day to day appearances, it's an endlessly creative movement, always moving to a new expression, sometimes radically different, but always at least a little different.

This movement has its own creative urge and everything has to be exactly what it is in any particular moment, because there is only this unexplainable happening.

The way this immediate happening is expressing itself is simply what it is. It is its own organizing tendency, its own formative urge.

A tomato plant doesn't have to worry about how to be a tomato plant; it's not deciding to be a tomato plant and it's not deciding how to behave like a tomato plant. It's simply an expression of nature or the universe.

The urge for that plant to be the plant that it is, is built into it; it is simply existence expressing itself the only way it can express itself.

We don't think a squirrel is deciding its career as a squirrel. We don't think a storm is deciding to be a storm. We don't think a bear is deciding whether or not to eat berries, or hibernate for the winter. We feel everything is driven by the forces of nature, the laws of existence.

We have the impression that everything is simply being the only thing it can be. Rocks, trees, weather conditions, plants, animals, planets, and so on, are expressions of the laws of the universe.

Universe simply means "undivided turning", one big movement. And its laws are simply its urge to move a certain way.

We generally believe that everything is an expression of nature, an expression of the universe. Everything except for one thing, "us".

There's a tendency to believe that human beings are not part of the natural world.

We generally believe that human beings are separate from the movement of nature, separate from the movement of the universe, and that we are in charge of our lives. We believe that we direct our lives and influence various things around us.

In other words, we believe that we move the universe, that we cause the universe to move in certain ways. Even though we never actually experience that.

Q: That's really strange. Why do we think that everything else is a movement of nature, but we're not? Why would I think I'm directing the universe, or that I'm creating myself?

DB: Christ had similar questions. He would ask people what the birds and flowers do to become what they are. He was pointing out that they don't do anything at all, they're simply expressions of the greater mystery of life.

He would then ask why anyone thought it was different for human beings.

There is no experience to indicate that we're causing ourselves to happen, or that we're deciding the course of our lives.

Q: So, again, if we look at our actual experience, there's just the happening of this moment. There isn't really any way to say what it is and we aren't making any of it happen. We don't even exist as anything separate from this happening.

In fact, I just realised, that's all any word can ultimately point to. It doesn't matter if it's a word like chair, or wall, or if it's a word like me, or you. All they can point to is an unexplainable happening.

DB: Yes. That's all any word can point to. The words may be useful for other things, but they can't explain what any of this actually is, or why it's happening the way it's happening.

As the Buddha pointed out, there is no self. There's just this happening, and no description really applies to it. He called it the *asankhata*, the "unformed". That's a Pali word.

He called himself the Tathagata, meaning one who has come to what actually is.

He stated that descriptions of physical forms, feelings, perceptions, mental activities, and states of consciousness, don't really apply to what actually is.

Q: But most us are focused on those descriptions, believing that those stories are true, a true understanding. And, with that understanding, we believe there's a "me" that is separate from life, a me that is causing things to happen.

From our actual experience, though, that isn't true; there's always only an immediate, unexplainable happening.

DB: Yes.

Q: Even talking about this is difficult, because I'm still having to use words like me and we, which give the impression of something other than this unexplainable happening.

DB: Yes, words are tricky. Basically, anytime we think or speak, we're in a fantasy, unless the belief in the stories has completely ended. Then the stories themselves are simply a mysterious happening.

Q: The stories themselves are a mysterious happening. Can you say more about that?

DB: Yes. Our descriptions of life are always false. The stories that say we're a person who understands life and directs life are not true.

If we believe those stories are true, then there is an endless obsession with them, a constant focus on them. However, if we see that those stories can never be true, then everything is simply a mysterious happening. Even the stories are simply a mysterious happening. We don't really know what they are.

They come up in certain situations, and can be useful as a tool, without ever being a true explanation for anything. And we don't have to be obsessed with them.

Q: So, with all of these considerations, you're saying our lives are totally out of control.

DB: No, I'm not saying that.

I'm saying that the idea of a self that is separate from existence, a self that is understanding existence and influencing its movement, is a fantasy. That self has never existed. There has never been any experience of that.

There's no self living in a world. That's a fantasy, merely a way of thinking about something that can't really be explained.

There's no self that's out of control. There never has been. There is always simply this immediate, unexplainable happening, doing what it does, being its own organizing urge.

It has its own way of expressing itself. All that has ever been is this immediate, unexplainable, liveliness, being its unexplainable urges.

Q: But most people don't look at everything as the natural expression of existence. Most of us are feeling that much of life is wrong, because we believe we're creating it. We believe that we create ourselves and much of the world, and we're not doing it very well.

We always have the idea that we need to correct ourselves, and the world, through our willpower, using our thoughts and understanding.

DB: Yes. That view is complex, confused, and conflicted. It's also totally false.

All there is, from actual experience, is this immediate, vibrant happening, simply happening automatically, spontaneously. Each moment just is what it is.

This happening, movement, flow, functioning, whatever you want to call it, is all that's happening, and it's happening automatically.

Q: You were very quickly labelled as a non-dual presenter when you first presented this, but you seem to be saying something very different from what most non-dual presenters are saying.

Most of them talk about consciousness, or awareness, saying that's what we really are.

DB: I know. And that's odd. Because even the traditional non-dual literature, like the *Ashtavakra Gita*, is saying that any idea of a knower, a knowing, and something known is a fantasy. It's saying that whatever this is, it can't really be described in any true way.

Q: *So there's no non-duality either.*

DB: No. That label is just as false as any other.

Q: *Then everything becomes unexplainable. But everything goes on presenting itself as usual, including the so-called stories. It's just that there's no belief in any of the stories, and everything is obviously occurring on its own.*

DB: Yes.

Q: *But if we stop believing that we understand life, or stop believing that we're making it happen, how does anything get done? We'll just sit around doing nothing.*

DB: Try it.

Try sitting here and never doing anything ever again. Try letting go of everything that you feel is valuable and useful. Try to stop thinking. Try to stop functioning.

Just try it, and you'll find out that you've never been making anything happen. You'll feel compelled to get up and do something. You won't sit here for the rest of your life.

You'll be active, but there's no you making that action happen. Instead, you're spontaneously compelled to act in some way. And your so-called thoughts will naturally arise as part of this happening.

Q: Again, that's a scary thing to consider.

DB: Yes, it may be frightening, at first. Contemplating these questions is important but, if we only focus on ideas, we'll never really open to this in a deep way. It's more important to feel this.

It's important to discover that there's nothing to be frightened of. So simply resting as this spontaneous happening, and feeling it happening spontaneously, is very important.

For that, we can sit down, or lie down, and simply be this happening, happening spontaneously.

In this experience, it may be realised that there never has been any understanding or personal doing. There is no self that is separate from this happening. There is no self making anything happen.

What we call "me" is simply this immediate, unexplainable occurrence. We don't exist as anything else.

Q: So, where does it go from that point?

DB: That's a bit trickier to discuss, because each of us is different. Remember that every apparent aspect of this undivided happening is different from every other aspect. It's like a tree. It's just one tree, but every portion of it is different from every other portion.

Even though this realisation is similar for anyone who seems to have it, it always arises in a different way and always expresses itself in a different way.

When I was talking about my own journey, I mentioned the consideration of where contentment can be found. Each of us will have to move in the direction that feels right to us.

It doesn't matter what anyone else says we should be doing: we have to move in whatever direction makes most sense to us, whatever feels right, in whatever way seems appropriate, and that's different for each person.

The fact that we're unique, different from everyone else, doesn't mean we have to live in isolation. We have to go in whatever direction makes most sense to us, but life will present people that are similar to us and we can find our place in the world with them.

But that requires being very honest with ourselves about what is most important to us, and what makes most sense. That may be very different from what others are telling us to be and do.

Q: That's never easy, going against popular opinion.

DB: No, that's not always easy, but to grow into our unique expression, our unique fullness, there will be growing pains.

Q: Yes, I've experienced some of those; my personal diary is filled with them. So, are there any more questions that you have to offer?

DB: No. Those are the essential ones. If you explore them thoroughly, you will probably find some interesting surprises.

Q: Yes, there's a lot to consider. There's a lot that is obvious right now, but I can feel there's much more to discover.

At this point, I don't really have anything more to ask. Is there anything more you want to add to this conversation?

DB: No. It feels like we've touched on all the important issues. I'm feeling pretty much talked out.

What I really need is a nap.

Acknowledgments and Appreciation

There isn't anyone who makes it through life alone. I'm grateful to so many people for their support.

To my brother Brent, for being the brother he is. Life has been a long strange journey for both of us.

To my mother and father, Gwen and Ed, for their love and care. They always did the best they could in raising their sons. Being a parent isn't easy.

To Shea Murphy, for our conversations, sharing things we don't share with others.

To Marcus, Linda, and Seren Fellowes, for my home away from home. Also, Marcus, the perfect accomplice, in roaming London day and night.

To Keith Millan and Dianne Wilt, for our shared meals, where we sort the world's problems. Also, for your support and company, when I had lost all community.

To Dale Purvis, for our Lyndale walks and talks, about everything under the sun, and beyond the sun.

To Link Phillips, for our Johnston Terminal mornings and the ongoing scrutiny of *Finnegans Wake*, the most amazing literary feat of all time.

To Valerie Metcalfe, for our friendship and the safety of your animal refuge.

To Mary Wall, for our friendship, and all that we learned together, when so much younger.

To Ross Davies, for our hanging out, over the years, from teenage angst to aching backs.

To Sandra Stuart, for your friendship, and for the early beginnings of this public sharing.

To Sally Perchaluk and Juliette Sabot, my loving, Catholic, connection.

To Bob Rogers, for our on-going, in-depth chinwags at the University coffee shop.

To Doug Phillips, for our on-going considerations, of how to tempt the secret urge, in everyone, to float among the clouds.

To Nick and Shakti Herzmark, for your friendship. Also, Nick, for our years of Dhamma combat, brothers in arms.

To Joe Forsyth, for your exuberant encouragement and a shared love of life's surprises. Big surprises.

To Jack Deyirmendjian, for our talks, and a shared love of clarity.

To Sheilagh Konyk, for reassuring me that I still looked normal on the outside, when it felt so strange on the inside.

To Jennifer Steen, Lynn-Marie Harper, and Enid Stevens, for our on-going connection, and your continued encouragement.

To Toan Tran, Jill Osler, Jon Mousely, and Norma Nickson.

To Sophie Rondeau, for sending my books to Joan Tollifson.

To Joan Tollifson, for your immediate, and generous, support, and for sending my books to Julian and Catherine.

To Julian and Catherine Noyce, for publishing my early works and this one too.

And last, but not least, thanks to those of you who read the first draft of this book and offered your impressions.

There are some who would ask, why thank anyone, if we're all just a mysterious flow, happening on its own? All I can say is that, in this great mixed bag of apparent things, I am grateful for every joyous aspect.

Current titles from
New Sarum Press

Real-World Nonduality - Various authors
The Ten Thousand Things - Robert Saltzman
The Joy of True Meditation - Jeff Foster
The Freedom to Love - Karin Visser

CONVERSATIONS ON NON-DUALITY

Twenty-Six Awakenings
edited by Eleanora Gilbert

The book explores the nature of true happiness, awakening, enlightenment and the 'Self' to be realised. It features 26 expressions of liberation, each shaped by different life experiences and offering a unique perspective.

The collection explores the different ways 'liberation' happened and 'suffering' ended. Some started with therapy or self-help workshops, or read books written by spiritual masters, while others travelled to exotic places and studied with gurus. Others leapt from the despair of addiction to drugs and alcohol to simply waking up unexpectedly to a new reality.

The 26 interviews included in the book are with: David Bingham, Daniel Brown, Sundance Burke, Katie Davis, Peter Fenner, Steve Ford, Jeff Foster, Suzanne Foxton, Gangaji, Richard Lang, Roger Linden, Wayne Liquorman, Francis Lucille, Mooji, Catherine Noyce, Jac O'Keeffe, Tony Parsons, Bernie Prior, Halina Pytlasinska, Genpo Roshi, Florian Schlosser, Mandi Solk, Rupert Spira, James Swartz, Richard Sylvester and Pamela Wilson.

CONSCIOUS.TV / Cherry Red Books

Printed in Poland
by Amazon Fulfillment
Poland Sp. z o.o., Wrocław